5 ingredient Slow Cooker Cookbook

Quick and Easy

5 Ingredient

Crock Pot Recipes

Louise Davidson

CONTENTS

INTRODUCTION

Have you ever found yourself going home, tired after a long day at work or school, only to discover that you still have to cook food? The prospect of having to prepare several ingredients, use a frying pan or an oven, and then perform other complicated and time consuming tasks may either make you to order out or skip dinner altogether. However, if think about it, using a slow cooker can solve this situation. It will make you save time and energy and money. What's not to like? On top of that, if you only need five ingredients to prepare your meals, and that's even better!

Slow cookers allow you to go home with food not only ready for you to eat, but also still tasty and warm at the same time. All you have to do is to prepare the ingredients in the morning, put all of them in the slow cooker and leave it. No mess, no dishes to clean, and not much effort compared to other kitchen appliances. This also means less work and faster preparation time. You arrive at home with a one-pot meal ready to eat. It will give you more time to enjoy your meal and to do other household tasks.

Compared to ovens, slow cookers require a significantly lower amount of electricity. This means lower bills for you to pay. Plus, ovens have a tendency to heat up not only the food, but also the entire kitchen. With slow cookers, you can prevent that.

Another money-saver is that with slow cookers, you can buy the less expensive, tougher meats. Instead of the expensive choice cuts, you can use the tougher meats because the slow cookers will make the meat more tender.

Because of how slow cooking works, flavors do not escape through smoke. The herbs, spices, stocks, and other flavorings circulate within the slow cooker. This retains and infuses more flavors when other appliances cannot.

Slow cookers save you a lot of time and coupled with my 5/15 rule, it will save you more time, energy, and money. **All recipes in this book will only have five ingredients or fewer. They will also require you fifteen minutes of preparation time at most.**

Take note that I don't count salt and pepper, water, and cooking spray as ingredients.

All the recipes included in this cookbook are easy to prepare. They only need a few ingredients and yet are very flavorful. They will surely please all the members of your family.

Bon appétit!

SLOW COOKER COOKING TIPS

Whenever you use your slow cooker, take note of the following tips to maximize its benefits:

Preparation

Meats must be thawed before they are placed in a slow cooker. When cooking chicken or turkey, it is a good idea to include the skin since this will help keep the meat moist and tender. One advantage of using slow cookers is that you can use tougher cuts that often cost less because, as cooking the meats for a long time tenderizes the meat.

Vegetables must be cut in the similar sizes so they can also be cooked at the same time. Since vegetables take more time to cook than meat, layering is important. Place vegetables on the bottom of the pot and faster cooking ingredients on the top.

Dry beans must be soaked and dried before putting them in a slow cooker. Using canned beans is a good idea since they have been soaked and boiled already.

Safety

You should still take precautions with your slow cooker. Do not fill it more than two thirds full, and keep it closed during the entire cooking process. If you have a new slow cooker, you should test it out first. Fill it with water, and then set it on low for eight hours. At the end of eight hours, take the temperature of the water with a food thermometer. Ideally, it should be 185° Fahrenheit. Anything lower or higher indicates a problem.

It's normal for the base of the slow cooker to heat up during cooking. It is designed not to exceed temperatures that could cause a fire. However, if you use the stoneware in a stove or store it in a fridge, it can crack. The stoneware is very sensitive to abrupt changes in temperature. If it is warm, do not set it on a cold table or pour cold water into it.

Cleaning

If your slow cooker is dishwasher safe, you can have the dishwasher do the cleaning for you. If not, do not immerse the slow cooker in water. Instead, use a sponge to clean it. If you have time, fill the stoneware with hot tap water and let it soak for two hours.

For stubborn marks, use baking soda. Use a sponge to scour the surface along with the powder. If this does not help, use ¼ cup of baking soda, a squirt of dish soap, fill the slow cooker with water that will cover all the marks, and then cook the solution for up to four hours.

At the same time, you can prevent these marks with slow cooker liners. These are heat-safe plastic liners that can save you the trouble of having to clean stubborn marks. You should use these when the recipes call for sugar-based sauces or cheese ingredients. Using a cooking spray will also help.

BREAKFAST

Apple Cinnamon Oatmeal

Serves: 4

Preparation time: 10 minutes

Cooking time: 1-2 hours on HIGH, 2-3 hours on LOW

Ingredients:

2 small apples, peeled, cored, and chopped

2 cup of rolled oats

4 cups of milk

1 tablespoon ground cinnamon

4 tablespoons of brown sugar

1 pinch of salt

1/3 cup raisins or any dried fruit (optional)

Directions:

- Place apples, oats, and milk into the crock-pot.
- Add brown sugar, cinnamon, and salt. Stir.
- Cook on HIGH for 1-2 hours or 2-3 hours on LOW.
- Always check consistency. Cook to your liking.
- Serve. Top with raisins or any dried fruit. (optional)

Nutrition (per serving)

Calories 300

Carbs 60 g

Protein 0 g

Sodium 100 mg

Bacon and Egg Casserole

Serves: 6-8

Preparation time: 15 minutes

Cooking time: 6 hours on LOW

Ingredients:

8 slices pre-cooked bacon

1 bell pepper, diced

1 onion, chopped

12 eggs

1 cup whole milk

Salt and ground black pepper

Cooking Spray

Directions:

- Spray the inside of the pot with cooking spray.
- Whisk eggs, salt, milk, and pepper in a bowl.
- Cook the onion and bell pepper in a skillet over medium heat until softened and fragrant, about 2-3 minutes. Remove from heat, and let cool down for a few minutes.
- Add onion, bell pepper, and bacon to the egg mixture.
- Pour the egg mixture into the slow cooker.
- Cook on LOW for about 6-8 hours, until the eggs are set and cooked.

Nutrition (per serving)

Calories 564

Carbs 13.2 g

Fat 132 g

Protein 156 g

Sodium 1488 mg

French Toast Casserole

Serves: 6

Preparation time: 30 minutes

Cooking time: 4 hours

Ingredients:

½ cup packed light brown sugar

7 large eggs

16 cinnamon-raisin bread (cut into 1-inch cubes (about 16 cups)

1 cup heavy cream

2 ½ cups whole milk

Non-stick cooking spray

2 cups pecans or walnuts (optional)

Directions:

- Tightly line your slow cooker with foil and coat with non-stick spray.
- Pour the bread cubes into the prepared slow cooker.
- Whisk together the milk, eggs, cream, and sugar (2 cups of pecan or walnuts, optional).
- Pour the egg mixture over the bread in a slow cooker, and push down the bread a bit so it can soak in the egg.
- Cover and cook on LOW for 4 hours.

Remove the top from the slow cooker, turn off the heat, and allow cooling for 15 minutes.

- Serve.

Nutrition (per serving)

Calories 149

Carbs 16 g

Fat 7 g

Protein 5 g

BEEF RECIPES

Beef Pot Roast

Serves: 4

Preparation time: 15 minutes

Cooking time: 6-7 hours on LOW

Ingredients:

1 8-ounce package sliced mushrooms

¼ cup ketchup

1-2 pounds boneless shoulder pot roast

1 green bell pepper, chopped

1 tablespoon Worcestershire sauce

Cooking Spray

¼ cup water

Salt and pepper

Directions:

- Put mushrooms and chopped bell pepper in the slow cooker.
- Coat with cooking spray.
- Combine water, ketchup, Worcestershire sauce, black pepper, and salt in a bowl. Stir until well blended.

- Coat a pan with cooking spray. Cook the meat for 5 minutes on medium-high heat until browned on all sides.
- Place roast in the slow cooker. Pour the sauce over the meat and vegetables. Cook on LOW for 6-7 hours

Nutrition (per serving)

Calories 623

Carbs 9.5 g

Fat 42.1 g

Protein 51.3g

Sodium 365 mg

Steak Pizzaiola

Serves: 4

Preparation time: 15 minutes

Cooking time: 7-8 hours on LOW

Ingredients:

1 ½ cup pasta sauce

¼ cup of water

1 medium-sized onion, sliced

1 bell pepper, sliced

1-2 lb. London broil steaks

Salt and pepper

Directions:

- Place all ingredients into the slow cooker.
- Season with salt and pepper.
- Cook on LOW for about 7-8 hours, flipping it once or twice.
- Serve with pasta, potatoes, bread or vegetables.

Nutrition (per serving)

Calories 273

Carbs 44 g

Fat 11 g

Protein 24 g

Sodium 433 mg

Chili Con Carne

Serves: 4

Preparation time: 15minutes

Cooking time: 4 – 6 hours on LOW

Ingredients:

1 10½ oz can hot-style vegetable juice

1 15½ oz can diced tomatoes

3 green chilies, undrained

1 pound ground beef

1 large onion, diced

15½ ounces water

Directions:

- On the stove, heat a skillet coated with cooking spray. Cook onions until meat is tender and brown. Add ground beef, and continue cooking until the meat is well cooked.
- Place the ground beef mixture, undrained tomatoes, beans, green chilies, and vegetable juice in the slow cooker.
- Add a full can of water using the diced tomato can. Stir and cover.
- Cook on LOW for 6-7 hours.

Nutrition (per serving)

Calories 449

Carbs 13.4 g

Fat 33.3 g

Protein 21.8 g

Sodium 442 mg

Creamy Swiss Steak

Serves: 4

Preparation time: 10minutes

Cooking time: 8-10 hours

Ingredients:

1 onion, diced

2 pounds round steak

2 cans, cream of mushroom soup

Salt and pepper

Directions:

- Place steak in crock pot. Season with salt and pepper
- Add diced onions.
- Pour soup over meat and onions.
- Cook on LOW for 8-10 hours.

Nutrition (per serving)

Calories 260

Carbs 14.1 g

Fat 28.9 g

Protein 74.2 g

Sodium 445 mg

Easy Beef Brisket

Serves: 4-6

Preparation time: 10 minutes

Cooking time: 6 hours

Ingredients:

2 cups chili sauce

1 can 12-oz regular Dr. Pepper

1 envelope dry onion soup mix

2 to 3 lb beef brisket

2 cups water

Directions:

- Cut beef brisket in half and place in crock pot.
- Mix onion soup mix, Dr. Pepper, water, and chili sauce.
- Pour mixture on brisket.
- Cover and place temperature on HIGH.
- Cook for 6 hours until meat is tender.
- Serve hot with your favorite vegetables

Nutrition (per serving)

Calories 474

Carbs 12.2 g

Fat 6 14.4 g

Protein 69.7 g

Sodium 2711 mg

Corned Beef and Cabbage

Serves: 6

Preparation time: 15 minutes

Cooking time: 5-6 Hours on HIGH

Ingredients:

½ cup water

3 pounds corned beef brisket with spice packet

2 medium yellow potatoes

1 medium onion, quartered

4 medium carrots, peeled

½ small head cabbage, cut into wedges

Directions:

- Sprinkle spices from packet evenly over meat.
- Place cabbage, onion, carrots, and potatoes in the slow cooker.
- Pour water over vegetables. Top with brisket.
- Cover and cook on LOW heat setting for 12 hours or on HIGH for 5 hours.
- Transfer meat to a cutting board. Let it rest for 10 minutes before slicing thinly against the grain.

Nutrition (per serving)

Calories 457

Carbs 16 g

Fat 27 g

Protein 44 g

Sodium 1600 mg

Spicy French Dip Beef Roast

Serves: 6

Preparation time: 10 minutes

Cooking time: 10 hours

Ingredients:

6 sandwich rolls

3 pounds of boneless beef roast, cut in thirds

½ cup dry Italian salad dressing mix

¼ cup water

2-oz can jalapeno peppers, diced, and drained

Directions:

- Place the 3 pieces of beef in slow cooker.
- Combine drained Italian dry dressing mix and water in a small bowl. Pour on beef.
- Cover and cook for 10 hours on LOW until beef is tender.
- Remove beef and shred. Place shredded beef back in slow cooker with cooking juices.
- Stir and serve on rolls.

Nutrition (per serving)

Calories 255

Carbs 21g

Fat 5 g

Protein 31 g

Sodium 598 mg

Cowboy Beef

Serves: 6

Preparation time: 15 minutes

Cooking time: 10-12 hours on LOW or 5-6 hours on HIGH

Ingredients:

2 pounds boneless beef chuck pot roast

1 teaspoon finely chopped canned chipotle pepper in adobo sauce

1 15-oz can chili beans in chili gravy

1 10-oz can diced tomatoes and green chilies, undrained

1 11-oz can whole kernel corn with sweet peppers, drained

Directions:

- Remove fat from meat. Place meat in slow cooker.
- In a medium bowl, combine chili beans in gravy, corn, tomatoes, green chilies, and chipotle pepper.
- Pour mixture over meat
- Cover and cook on LOW for 10-12 hours or on HIGH 5-6 hours.

- Transfer meat to a cutting board, Slice meat. Arrange in a serving dish. Using a slotted spoon, spoon bean mixture over meat.

Nutrition (per serving)

Calories 307

Carbs 23 g

Fat 7 g

Protein 18 g

Sodium 655 mg

Ranch Seasoned Beef

Serves: 4

Preparation time: 15 minutes

Cooking time: 8 hours on LOW

Ingredients:

1 packet ranch seasoning for salad such as Hidden Valley Ranch Packet

3 lbs beef chuck pot roast, boneless and cut into large cubes

Cooking Spray

3 garlic cloves, minced

½ cup water

1/3 cup white vinegar

1 large sweet onion, sliced

Salt and pepper

Directions:

- Spray crock pot with cooking spray.
- Season the beef with salt and pepper. Place beef in the slow cooker.
- Add sliced onions.
- Mix ranch packet, garlic, water, and vinegar. Pour on beef.
- Cook on LOW for 8 hours.

Nutrition (per serving)

Calories 322

Carbs 28 g

Fat 30 g

Protein 14 g

Sodium 670 mg

CHICKEN AND TURKEY RECIPES

BBQ Cheesy Chicken Bacon Sandwich

Serves: 6

Preparation time: 15minutes

Cooking time: 4 hours on HIGH

Ingredients:

4 large boneless chicken breasts

2 cups BBQ sauce

2 cups shredded cheddar cheese

8 large onion rolls/buns

6 bacon strips, pre-cooked

Salt and pepper

Cooking spray

Directions:

- Spray slow cooker with cooking spray.
- Season chicken breasts with salt and pepper. Place chicken breasts in the slow cooker.
- Pour BBQ sauce on top.
- Cook on HIGH for 4 hours or 7-8 hours on LOW.
- Shred chicken.

- Place chicken back in slow cooker. Top with the shredded cheese. Slow cook for about 10 more minutes until the cheese is melted.
- Place cheesy chicken in bun. Top with bacon strips and serve.

Nutrition (per serving)

Calories 269

Carbs 63.7 g

Fat 29.9 g

Protein 47.5 g

Sodium 1960 mg

Sesame-Ginger Turkey Wraps

Serves: 6

Preparation time: 20 minutes

Cooking time: 6-7 hours on LOW, 3-3 ½ hours on HIGH

Ingredients:

2 skinless turkey thighs, about 2 pounds

⅛ cup water

1 8-oz bag of broccoli slaw mix

½ cup sesame-ginger stir-fry sauce

6 8-inch flour tortillas

3 green onions, diced

Non-stick cooking spray

Directions:

- Lightly coat a slow cooker with cooking spray. Placed turkey.
- In a small bowl, stir together stir-fry sauce and water. Pour over turkey.
- Cover and cook on LOW for 6-7 hours or on HIGH for 3-3 ½ hours.
- Transfer turkey to a cutting board. Cool slightly. Remove turkey from bones. Discard bones. Shred turkey. Return to mixture to the slow cooker. Stir broccoli into mixture in cooker. Cover and let stand for 5 minutes.

- To serve, place some turkey mixture on each tortilla. Top with green onions. Roll up and serve.

Nutrition (per serving)

Calories 207

Carbs 21g

Fat 5 g

Carbs 20g

Protein 20 g

Sodium 422 mg

Chicken Curry

Serves: 6

Preparation time: 15 minutes

Cooking time: 10 hours on LOW

Ingredients:

1 tablespoon curry powder

14-oz can low sodium chicken broth

2 medium onions, chopped

1½ boneless, skinless chicken thighs, quartered

4 potatoes, peeled and cut into chunks

Directions:

- Place all ingredients in slow cooker.
- Cover and cook on LOW for 8-10 hours, or on HIGH 5 hours.
- Cook until chicken is tender but not dry.
- Serve hot.

Nutrition (per serving)

Calories 367

Carbs 40 g

Fat 5 g

Protein 41 g

Sodium 1160 mg

BBQ Turkey Breast

Serves: 6

Preparation time: 10 minutes

Cooking time: 5-7- hours on LOW

Ingredients:

1 turkey breast, about 5-6 pounds, thawed and rinsed
under cold water

1 large onion, cut into chunks

Gravy or BBQ sauce for serving

½ cup of barbecue spice rub

3 tbsp butter, at room temperature

Directions:

- Mix butter and barbecue spices in small bowl.
- Coat turkey breast with butter mixture, pressing it and pushing some under the skin.
- Place onion chunks inside the turkey's cavity. Place the turkey skin side up in slow cooker.
- Cook on LOW for 5-7 hours.
- Serve with gravy or barbecue sauce.

Nutrition (per serving)

Calories 308

Carbs 14 g

Fat 14.7 g

Protein 13.3 g

Sodium 1382 mg

Citrus infused Chicken Breasts

Serves: 2-4

Preparation time: 10 minutes

Cooking time: 3 hours on HIGH or 6 hours on LOW

Ingredients:

1 tablespoon of lemon pepper seasoning

1 can cream of chicken soup

Juice of half a lemon

2 large oranges, 1 juiced, 1 sliced

4 boneless and skinless chicken breasts

Salt and pepper

Cooking spray

Water

Directions:

- Grease the bottom of the slow cooker with cooking spray.
- Season the chicken breasts with salt and pepper.
- Place the orange slices at the bottom of the slow cooker. Let the chicken breasts sit on the oranges.
- Pour the soup in a bowl, add lemon and orange juice and lemon pepper.

- Add ½ can of water to the mix. Whisk until well combined.
- Pour it over the chicken in the slow cooker.
- Cook for 3 hours on HIGH or 6 hours on LOW.
- Serve with your favorite vegetables and rice.

Nutrition (per serving)

Calories 670

Carbs 34.52 g

Fat 37.07 g

Protein 45.31 g

Sodium 1809 mg

Garlic-Infused Turkey Breast

Serves: 4-6

Preparation time: 15 minutes

Cooking time: 10 hours

Ingredients:

2 quartered medium onions

2 heads of garlic cloves

½ cup water

1 bone-in turkey breast, about 5-6 pounds

Salt and pepper to taste

2 tablespoons butter, at room temperature

Directions:

- Prepare garlic by peeling the cloves. There should be around 20 cloves. Smash about half of the cloves with a large blade. Set aside.
- Rinse turkey thoroughly under running water, and pat dry with paper towels.
- Sprinkle turkey with salt and pepper. Rub the butter all over the turkey's skin and under the skin.
- Place smashed garlic in the turkey breast cavity.
- Place in slow cooker. Add water on the side of the slow cooker to cover the bottom.

- Add onion and remaining garlic around the side of cooker and cover.
- Cook on LOW for 9-10 hours.
- Remove from slow cooker, and let stand for 15 minutes before slicing.

Nutrition (per serving)

Calories 359

Carbs 6.6 g

Fat 39.8 g

Protein 82 g

Sodium 519 mg

Tropical-Favored Chicken

Serves: 6

Preparation time: 15 minutes

Cooking time: 6 hours

Ingredients:

3 medium-sized sweet potatoes

1 whole large chicken, cut in pieces

1 20-oz can pineapple chunks, in juice

2 cups can chicken broth

2 tablespoons cornstarch

2 tablespoons cold water

Directions:

- Wash, peel, and cube sweet potatoes.
- Place cut-up chicken in slow cooker.
- Place the sweet potatoes over the chicken in the slow cooker.
- Pour chicken broth in the slow cooker.
- Add the pineapples and juice on top.
- Cover and cook on LOW for 6 hours, or until chicken and potatoes are tender.
- Mix cornstarch and water until smooth just before serving. Stir cornstarch paste into cooker. Cook

for an additional 8-10 minutes, until sauce
thickens.

Nutrition (per serving)

Calories 517

Carbs 40 g

Fat 8.5 g

Protein 67 g

Sodium 732 mg

Italian Seasoned Chicken with Spinach and Pasta

Serves: 4

Preparation time: 15 minutes

Cooking time: 6 hours and 15 minutes on LOW

Ingredients:

4 large boneless and skinless chicken breasts

1 10-oz can of cream of chicken soup

1 package of dry Italian seasoning mix for salad

1 8-oz fresh baby spinach leaves, washed

1 package of penne pasta

Salt and pepper

Cooking spray

Directions:

- Spray the bottom and sides of the slow cooker with cooking spray.
- Place chicken breast in the slow cooker. Season with salt and pepper.
- Mix soup and Italian dressing together.
- Pour over top of chicken.
- Cover and cook on LOW for 6 hours.
- Remove the chicken breast, and shred or cut the chicken into bite-sized pieces.

- Place the chicken back in the slow cooker.
- Place spinach over the chicken breasts.
- Cook for an additional 15 minutes, or until the spinach is cooked.
- Stir a few times to coat in the sauce.
- To serve, cook the pasta according to package instruction.
- Serve the chicken and spinach over cooked pasta.

Nutrition (per serving)

Calories 361

Carbs 42 g

Fat 12 g

Protein 25 g

Sodium 1657 mg

Barbecue Sweet Gold Chicken Drumsticks

Serves: 4

Preparation time: 15 minutes

Cooking time: 6-8 hours on LOW or 3-4 hours on HIGH

Ingredients:

1 large sweet onion, cut into ¾-inch thick slices

2½ pounds chicken drumsticks, skinned

1 cup barbecue sauce

2 tablespoons orange marmalade

2 tablespoons yellow mustard

Salt and pepper

Olive oil

Directions:

- Generously brush the bottom and sides of the slow cooker with olive oil.
- Place the sliced onion on the bottom.
- Add chicken on top of the onions. Season with salt and pepper.
- For the sauce: Stir together BBQ sauce, marmalade, and mustard in a small bowl.
- Add the sauce on top of the chicken.

- Cover and cook on LOW for 6-8 hours or on HIGH for 3-4 hours.
- Serve chicken with sauce.

Nutrition (per serving)

Calories 456

Carbs 37 g

Fat 17 g

Protein 38 g

Sodium 963 mg

Creamy Mexican Chicken

Serves: 4

Preparation time: 10 minutes

Cooking time: 4 hours 30 minutes

Ingredients:

5 boneless chicken breasts

1 15½-oz can corn

1 15-oz jar salsa

1 8-oz package cream cheese, cut into chunks

1 15½-oz can black beans

Cooking spray

Salt and pepper

Directions:

- Spray slow cooker with cooking spray.
- Place boneless chicken breasts into slow cooker. Season with salt and pepper.
- Add salsa, black beans, and drained corn.
- Cover. Put on HIGH for 4 hours.
- Add cream cheese, and let it sit for ½ hour. Or until the cream cheese has melted.
- Serve.

Nutrition (per serving)

Calories 308

Carbs 48 g

Fat 34.2 g

Protein 68.3 g

Sodium 1036 mg

Chicken Teriyaki

Serves: 4

Preparation time: 15minutes

Cooking time: 7-8 hours

Ingredients:

½ cup chicken broth

1 cup teriyaki sauce

5 boneless chicken breasts, cut into strips

2 8-oz cans crushed pineapple with juice

3 tablespoons soy sauce

Cooking spray

Salt and pepper

Directions:

- Spray slow cooker's bottom and sides with cooking spray.
- Place chicken in slow cooker. Season generously with salt and pepper.
- Mix together in a bowl, the teriyaki sauce, crushed pineapple with juice, and soya sauce. Pour over chicken.
- Cover and cook on LOW for 7-8 hours.
- Serve.

Nutrition (per serving)

Calories 288

Carbs 19.19 g

Fat 32.0 g

Protein 39 g

Sodium 1430 mg

Quick and Easy Chicken Broccoli Casserole

Serves: 6

Preparation time: 10 minutes

Cooking time: 6-7 hours

Ingredients:

5 boneless chicken breasts

1 can cream of broccoli with cheese soup

½ cup chicken broth

1 6-oz package of stuffing for chicken, such as Stove Top

1 10-oz bag frozen, chopped broccoli, thawed

Cooking spray

Salt and pepper

Directions:

- Spray slow cooker with cooking spray.
- Place chicken in the bottom of the slow cooker. Season with salt and pepper.
- Mix all remaining ingredients in a bowl, and pour on top of chicken.
- Cover and cook on LOW for 6-7 hours.

Nutrition (per serving)

Calories 280

Carbs 18.7 g

Fat 13 g

Protein 45.4 g

Sodium 992 mg

PORK RECIPES

Simple Pork Meatballs in Tomato Sauce

Serves: 6-8

Preparation time: 15 minutes

Cooking time: 8 hours

Ingredients:

1 egg, beaten

1 28-oz can of tomato sauce

1 16-oz can crushed tomatoes

1 medium yellow onion, chopped

1½ pounds ground pork

½ cup water

Salt and pepper

Directions:

- Mix ground pork, egg, water, and onion in a medium-sized bowl.
- Season generously with salt and pepper.
- Shape mixture into about 20-24 meatballs.
- Mix the crushed tomatoes and spaghetti sauce in the slow cooker.
- Place meatballs into the sauce mixture.
- Cook on LOW for 8 hours.

Nutrition (per serving)

Calories 186

Carbs 14.9 g

Fat 20.7 g

Protein 35.3 g

Sodium 953 mg

Peachy Sweet Pork

Serves: 6

Preparation time: 15minutes

Cooking time: 7 hours on LOW

Ingredients:

2 sweet potatoes

3 peach, pitted, peeled and diced

½ cup water

½ cup peach preserves jelly

1 teaspoon cumin

2 pork loins, about 1½ pounds each

Salt and Pepper

Cooking spray

Directions:

- Spray slow cooker with non-stick spray.
- Place pork in slow cooker. Season with salt and pepper.
- Place the sweet potatoes around the pork.
- Stir together the peach preserves, water, and cumin. Pour the sauce over the pork and potatoes.
- Cook on LOW for 7 hours.

Nutrition (per serving)

Calories 511

Carbs 18 g

Fat 29 g

Protein 44 g

Sodium 1724 mg

Split Peas with Ham

Serves: 8

Preparation time: 15 minutes

Cooking time: 4 hours

Ingredients:

1 medium onion, chopped

4 medium carrots, diced

8 medium ham hocks, about 4 oz each

2½ quarts boiling water

1 pound dry yellow split peas

Salt and Pepper

Directions:

- Bring water to a boil in a saucepan.
- Place ingredients into slow cooker.
- Add boiling water and stir together.
- Cover and cook on HIGH for 4 hours or on LOW for 7-8 hours until vegetables are tender.
- Remove the ham hocks from the slow cooker when cooked. Debone the meat. Stir cut-up chunks of meat back into the slow cooker before serving.

Nutrition (per serving)

Calories 271

Carbs 16.5 g

Fat 35.6 g

Protein19 g

Sodium 321 mg

Root Beer Pulled Pork Sandwich

Serves: 4

Preparation time: 10 minutes

Cooking time: 7-8 hours on LOW

Ingredients:

1-2 cans root beer soda

2 cups BBQ sauce, plus some more for serving

2 pork loins, about 1 – 1 ½ pounds

Salt and Pepper

½ cup prepared slaw

4 rolls

Directions:

- Season the pork loins with pepper and salt.
- Place pork in slow cooker, and pour enough root beer and BBQ sauce to almost cover it.
- Cook on LOW for 7-8 hours.
- Remove pork and discard liquid.
- Shred the pork.
- To serve, warm the sandwich rolls. Add shredded pork with some barbecue sauce. Top with slaw.
- Serve warm.

Nutrition (per serving)

Calories 446

Carbs 88.7 g

Fat 18.3 g

Protein 21.8 g

Sodium 1847 mg

Smoky Baby Back Ribs

Serves: 4

Preparation time: 10 minutes

Cooking time: 5 hours on HIGH and 10 minutes on the grill

Ingredients:

2 baby back pork ribs racks, halved

1 cup barbecue sauce

1 teaspoon of liquid smoke (optional)

4 tablespoons barbecue spices mix

Cooking spray

Directions:

- Remove the membrane and excess fat from the ribs.
- Rub each rib half rack with 1 tablespoon of the barbecue spice mix.
- Spray slow cooker with cooking spray.
- Place pork ribs in slow cooker.
- Combine the barbecue sauce and liquid smoke. Brush the racks lightly with half of the liquid smoke and barbecue sauce mix.
- Cook on HIGH for 5 hours until tender.

- When ready to serve, remove ribs from slow cooker, and place them on a foil lined baking dish. Brush ribs with remaining barbecue sauce.
- Broil the ribs in the oven for about 5-10 minutes. Watch carefully so they don't burn. This can also be done on the barbecue grill.
- Serve warm with your favorite side dishes.

Nutrition (per serving)

Calories 682

Carbs 21 g

Fat 43 g

Protein 56 g

Sodium 811 mg

Apple Polish Sausage Bites

Serves: 4

Preparation time: 10 minutes

Cooking time: 6-8 hours on LOW

Ingredients:

¾ cup brown sugar

4 cloves garlic, minced

6 fully cooked Polish sausages like Polska Kielbasa, cut into 1-inch pieces

1-2 pinches red pepper flakes

1 cup chunky unsweetened applesauce

Salt and pepper

Directions:

- Spray the slow cooker with cooking spray.
- Place all ingredients in a slow cooker. Season with salt and pepper.
- Cover and cook for 6-8 hours on LOW until the sausages are tender
- Stir a few times.
- Serve.

Nutrition (per serving)

Calories 332

Carbs 6.8 g

Fat 20 g

Protein 9 g

Sodium 678 mg

Seasoned Pork Chops

Serves: 4

Preparation time: 10 minutes

Cooking time: 6 hours

Ingredients:

4 large pork chops

1 16-oz bottle of Italian herb dressing

Slow cooker liner, such as parchment paper

Directions:

- Line the slow cooker with a liner.
- Place pork chops into the slow cooker.
- Pour entire bottle of dressing over the pork chops.
- Cook for 6 hours on LOW.
- Serve.

Nutrition (per serving)

Calories 286

Carbs 0 g

Fat 13 g

Protein 39 g

Sodium 640 mg

Apricot-Glazed Pork Roast

Serves: 6

Preparation time: 10 minutes

Cooking time: 6 hours

Ingredients:

1 medium onion, chopped

1 tablespoon Dijon mustard

1 cup apricot preserves

¾ cup chicken broth

2 pounds boneless pork loin roast

Salt and pepper

Cooking spray

Directions:

- In a medium-sized bowl, mix broth, mustard, and onion.
- Place roast in slow cooker.
- Pour broth mixture over meat.
- Cover and cook on LOW for 5-6 hours, until tender.

Nutrition (per serving)

Calories 298

Carbs 9.5 g

Fat 15.5 g

Protein 33 g

Sodium 314 mg

Apple Sauce Pork Roast

Serves: 4

Preparation time: 10 minutes

Cooking time: 8-9 hours on LOW

Ingredients:

1-2 pinch cinnamon to taste

1½ cups unsweetened applesauce

2 pounds pork loin roast

1 teaspoon dry thyme

Salt and pepper

Cooking spray

Directions:

- Spray the slow cooker bottom and sides with cooking spray.
- Place pork roast in slow cooker. Sprinkle with the thyme, and season with salt and pepper.
- Pour a generous amount of unsweetened applesauce over the pork.
- Sprinkle with cinnamon.
- Cook on LOW for 8-9 hours, until the pork is well cooked.

Nutrition (per serving)

Calories 212

Carbs 3.8 g

Fat 6.8 g

Protein 31.2 g

Sodium 247 mg

Shredded Pork for Tacos

Serves: 4

Preparation time: 15 minutes

Cooking time: 8-10 hours on LOW + 15 minutes

Ingredients:

1 cup chicken broth

2 pounds boneless pork shoulder roast

1½ cup enchilada sauce

8-12 flour tortillas or taco shells

Different kinds of toppers, like lettuce, cheese, diced
tomato, guacamole.

Directions:

- Place pork in slow cooker.
- Add broth.
- Cover and cook on LOW for 8-10 hours.
- Remove meat from cooker. Discard broth. Shred meat.
- Place the shredded pork back in the slow cooker with the enchilada sauce. Continue cooking on low for 15 minutes.
- Warm flour tortillas or taco shells according to package directions.

- To assemble, place pork mixture in center of warm tortillas. Top with your favorite toppings like lettuce, cheese, diced tomatoes and guacamole.

Nutrition (per serving)
Calories 616

Carbs 20 g

Fat 13 g

Protein 61 g

Sodium 846 mg

Bean Soup with Shredded Pork

Serves: 8

Preparation time: 10 minutes

Cooking time: 4-6 hours on LOW

Ingredients:

8 thick cut pork chops

1 medium-sized, finely chopped onion

1 tablespoon adobo sauce

4 cloves garlic, chopped

1 pound dried black beans, rinsed

1 teaspoon salt

5 cups of water

Directions:

- Combine pork chops, beans, garlic, adobo sauce, salt, and onion in slow cooker.
- Add 5 cups of water.
- Cook on LOW until pork chops and beans are tender for 4-6 hours.
- Remove bones from pork. Shred meat.
- Add meat back to slow cooker with beans.
- Season with salt.
- Serve.

Nutrition (per serving)

Calories 238

Carbs 47.2 g

Fat 2.3 g

Protein 13.0 g

Sodium 440 mg

FISH AND SEAFOOD RECIPES

Garlic Butter Tilapia

Serves: 4

Preparation time: 15 minutes

Cooking time: 2 hours

Ingredients:

2 tablespoons butter, at room temperature

2 garlic cloves, minced

 2 teaspoons flat parsley, chopped

4 tilapia fillets

1 lemon, cut into wedges

Salt and Pepper to taste

Cooking spray

Directions:

- Place a large sheet of aluminum foil on a work surface. Place fillets in the middle.
- Place in a slow cooker.
- Season generously with salt and pepper.
- Mix butter with minced garlic and chopped parsley. Evenly spread mixture over each fillet.

- Wrap foil around fish, sealing all sides.
- Cook on HIGH for 2 hours.
- Serve with lemon wedges.

Nutrition (per serving)

Calories 89

Carbs 0.5 g

Fat 9.8 g

Protein 8.4 g

Sodium 202 mg

Fish Chowder

Serves: 6

Preparation time: 15 minutes

Cooking time: 7 hours

Ingredients:

1 lb frozen cod fillets

1 teaspoon lemon pepper

1 onion, chopped

2 large potatoes finely chopped

1 10-oz can cream of celery soup

1½ cups water

Salt and pepper

Directions:

- Fry onions in a skillet with cooking spray for about 2 minutes, or until tender and fragrant.
- Place potatoes and onions in slow cooker. Season with salt and pepper.
- Add water, cream soup, and seasonings. Stir to mix well.
- Cut fish fillets in half, and place on top of other ingredients.
- Cover. Cook on LOW for 7-8 hours.
- Do not stir during cooking time.

- Break fish into chunks.
- Serve.

Nutrition (per serving)

Calories 211

Carbs 15 g

Fat 11 g

Protein 13 g

Sodium 484 mg

Buttery Salmon with Onions and Carrots

Serves: 4

Preparation time: 15 minutes

Cooking time: 7-9 hours on LOW

Ingredients:

4 salmon fillets

4 tablespoons butter

4 onions, chopped

16 oz baby carrots

3 cloves garlic, minced

Salt and pepper

Directions:

- Melt butter in the microwave, and pour into the slow cooker.
- Add onions, garlic, and baby carrots.
- Cover and cook for 6-7 hours on LOW, stirring occasionally until vegetables begin to caramelize.

- Place fillet over vegetables in slow cooker, and season with salt and pepper.
- Cover and cook on LOW for 1-2 hours until salmon flakes.
- Serve on a serving plate, and top with onion mixture.

Nutrition (per serving)

Calories 367

Carbs 12.2 g

Fat 22 g

Protein 39 g

Sodium 1090 mg

Scalloped Potatoes with Salmon

Serves: 4

Preparation time: 15 minutes

Cooking time: 7-8 hours on LOW

Ingredients:

3 tablespoons all-purposed flour

1 10¾-oz can of cream of mushroom soup

5 medium-sized potatoes, peeled, and sliced

1 16-oz can of salmon, drained and flaked

½ cup chopped onions

¼ cup water

Salt and pepper

Cooking spray

Directions:

- Generously spray the slow cooker bottom and sides with cooking spray.
- Place half of the potatoes in slow cooker.
- Sprinkle with half of the flour, then season with salt and pepper.
- Cover with half the flaked salmon, then sprinkle with half the onions.
- Repeat layers.

- Combine soup and water. Pour over top of potato and salmon mixture.
- Cover and cook on LOW for 7-8 hours or until potatoes are tender.

Nutrition (per serving)

Calories 367

Carbs 5.2 g

Fat 22 g

Protein 39

Sodium 849 mg

VEGETARIAN RECIPES

Kidney Bean Veggie Chili

Serves: 4

Preparation time: 10 minutes

Cooking time: 6-7 hours on LOW

Ingredients:

1 15.5-oz can of kidney beans

1 28-oz can crushed tomatoes

1 small can tomato paste

2 green bell peppers, diced

1 tablespoon chili powder

1 cup water

Salt and pepper

Directions:

- Place all ingredients in slow cooker.
- Cover and cook for 6-7 hours on LOW.
- Serve over rice or cooked pasta.

Nutrition (per serving)

Calories 53

Carbs 9.2 g

Fat 1.8 g

Protein 8 g

Sodium 440 mg

Vegetable Rice

Serves: 4-8

Preparation time: 10 minutes

Cooking time: 2 hours

Ingredients:

2 cups low sodium vegetable stock

3 shallots, diced

1½ cups frozen vegetables mix

2 tablespoons low-sodium soya sauce

1 cup long grain brown rice

Cooking spray

Salt and pepper

Directions:

- Fry shallots in a non-stick skillet coated with cooking spray until tender, about 2 minutes.
- Coat slow cooker with non-stick cooking spray.
- Place all ingredients in slow cooker.
- Cover and cook for 2 hours on LOW, until rice is tender.

Nutrition (per serving)

Calories 120

Carbs 24.9 g

Fat 1.0 g

Protein 2.9 g

Sodium 405 mg

Vegetarian Gumbo

Serves: 6

Preparation time: 10 minutes

Cooking time: 6-8 hours on LOW

Ingredients:

2 cups frozen, cut okra, thawed

2 teaspoons Cajun seasoning

2 15-oz cans black beans, rinsed and drained

1 16-oz package frozen diced sweet peppers and onions

1 28-oz can diced fire-roasted tomatoes, undrained

Directions:

- Combine all the ingredients in the slow cooker.
- Cover and cook for 6-8 hours on LOW.
- Serve.

Nutrition (per serving)

Calories 153

Carbs 31 g

Fat 0.8 g

Protein 12 g

Sodium 639 mg

Artichoke Pasta

Serves: 6

Preparation time: 15 minutes

Cooking time: 6 hours on LOW or 3 hours on HIGH

Ingredients:

12 oz dry linguine or fettuccine

3 14-oz tomatoes, diced with basil, garlic, and oregano

1 14-oz cans artichoke hearts, drained

1 tablespoon minced garlic

½ cup heavy cream

Cooking spray

Directions:

- Coat the inside of slow cooker with non-stick cooking spray.
- Drain 2 of the cans of diced tomatoes.
- Combine drained and undrained tomatoes, garlic, and artichoke hearts in the slow cooker.
- Cover and cook for 6-8 hours on LOW or 3-4 hours on HIGH.
- Stir the cream.
- Cook pasta according to package directions; drain.

- Serve artichoke sauce over hot cooked pasta.

Nutrition (per serving)

Calories 403

Carbs 68 g

Fat 1 g

Protein 13 g

Sodium 1513 mg

DESSERT RECIPES

Chocolate Cake

Serves: 4

Preparation time: 10 minutes

Cooking time: 3 hours on HIGH, 6 hours on LOW

Ingredients:

1 box instant Chocolate Pudding Mix

4 eggs

1 box Chocolate or Devil's Food Cake Mix

8 oz sour Cream

¾ cup vegetable oil

1 cup water

Cooking spray

Directions:

- Coat the slow cooker with cooking spray.
- Mix all the remaining ingredients together, and pour into slow cooker.
- Cook on HIGH for 3 hours or on LOW for 6 hours.

Nutrition (per serving)

Calories 605

Carbs 46 g

Fat 43 g

Protein 8 g

Sodium 637 mg

Monkey Bread

Serves: 6

Preparation time: 15 minutes

Cooking time: 2 hours

Ingredients:

1 teaspoon cinnamon

1 cup brown sugar

¼ cup butter, melted

1 tube biscuits like Pillsbury Biscuits

Directions:

- Break biscuits into the pre-cut pieces.
- Mix the brown sugar and cinnamon.
- Dip biscuit pieces into melted butter.
- Put buttered biscuit into a bowl of cinnamon and brown sugar until fully coat.
- Place the pieces into slow cooker until you have all of the pieces layered in the slow cooker.
- Pour extra brown sugar and cinnamon on top.
- Cook on LOW for 2 hours.
- Serve.

Nutrition (per serving)

Calories 368

Carbs 68.1 g

Fat 9.2 g

Protein 5.1 g

Sodium 1071 mg

Peach Dump Cake

Serves: 6

Preparation time: 10 minutes

Cooking time: 4 hours

Ingredients:

4 cups frozen peaches

2 eggs

6 tablespoons butter, melted

1 (18.25 oz) box yellow cake mix

¼ teaspoon cinnamon

½ cup water

Directions:

- Place frozen peaches in the bottom of the slow cooker.
- Mix the cake mix with eggs, water and butter until smooth.
- Spoon the batter over the peaches.
- Sprinkle with cinnamon.
- Cook for 4 hours on HIGH.
- Serve warm.

Nutrition (per serving)

Calories 211

Carbs 21 g

Fat 23.4 g

Protein 6.8 g

Sodium 676 mg

Caramel Flan

Serves: 4

Preparation time: 20 minutes

Cooking time: 4 hours on HIGH

Ingredients:

3 large eggs

1½ cups whole milk

½ tablespoon vanilla extract

1¼ cups granulated sugar, divided

8oz. can sweetened condensed milk

Hot water

Directions:

- Warm a small saucepan on the stove over medium heat. Pour in 1 cup sugar.
- Stir until sugar melts. Remove from the heat, and spoon evenly the liquid caramel into each of 4 ramekins. Set aside.
- Whisk eggs in a large bowl. Add condensed and whole milk, and the remaining ¼ cup sugar. Strain the mixture through cheesecloth. Pour over caramel in the ramekins.
- Set the ramekins in the slow cooker. Carefully pour in hot water to surround them.

- Cover and cook for 4 hours on HIGH.
- Carefully lift out the flans, and let them cool on a wire rack for an hour.
- Serve. Run a knife around the edge of each ramekin and flip the chilled flans upside down into serving plates.

Nutrition (per serving)

Calories 223

Carbs 35 g

Fat 6 g

Protein 7 g

Sodium 481 mg

CONCLUSION

Thank you for taking the time to read about slow cookers and the many recipes that you can use. I hope you enjoy the recipes not only for yourself but also for your family, friends, and other loved ones.

Good cooking does not need to take too much of your time or require a lot of ingredients to taste amazing. You can still have the flavors and the dining experience that you want even with only 5 ingredients and with only 15 minutes to prepare for it. I hope this book and the recipes in it, along with your slow cooker, will give you one of your best home-cooked meals today.

ABOUT THE AUTHOR

Louise Davidson is an avid cook who likes simple flavors and easy-to-make meals. She lives in Tennessee with her husband, her three grown children, her two dogs, and the family's cat Whiskers. She loves the outdoor and has mastered the art of camp cooking on open fires and barbecue grills.

In colder months, she loves to whip up some slow cooker meals, and uses her favorite cooking tools in her kitchen, the cast iron pans, and Dutch oven. She also is very busy preparing Christmas treats for her extended family and friends. She gets busy baking for the holiday season sometimes as early as October. Her recipes are cherished by everyone who has tasted her foods and holiday treats.

Louise is a part-time writer of cookbooks, sharing her love of food, her experience, and her family's secret recipes with her readers.

She also loves to learn and share tips and tricks to make life.

Other books from Louise include:

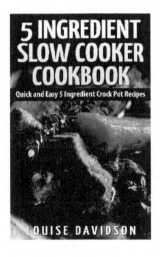

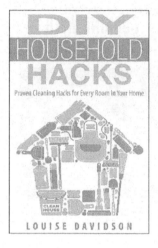

APPENDIX

Cooking Conversion Charts

1. Volumes

US Fluid Oz.	US	US Dry Oz.	Metric Liquid ml
¼ oz.	2 tsp.	1 oz.	10 ml.
½ oz.	1 tbsp.	2 oz.	15 ml.
1 oz.	2 tbsp.	3 oz.	30 ml.
2 oz.	¼ cup	3½ oz.	60 ml.
4 oz.	½ cup	4 oz.	125 ml.
6 oz.	¾ cup	6 oz.	175 ml.
8 oz.	1 cup	8 oz.	250 ml.

Tsp.= teaspoon - tbsp.= tablespoon – oz.= ounce – ml.= millimeter

2. Oven Temperatures

Celsius (ºC)*	Fahrenheit (ºF)
90	220
110	225
120	250
140	275
150	300
160	325
180	350
190	375
200	400
215	425
230	450
250	475
260	500

*Rounded numbers